A WORKBOOK FOR POVERTY BY AMERICA:

Overview, Analysis And Definitions. A Guide to Matthew Desmond's Book.

Contents

OVERVIEW, ANALYSIS AND DEFINITIONS

Someone had recently discovered an analysis in that painted a considerably more upbeat image of the income distribution in the United States, he claimed. How is this possible considering that I claimed there were at least 50,000,000 poor people in this country?

I read the essay. The same fundamental study that I was citing was used in the essay. The difference was in point of view. The middle third of American society—the organized worker in well-paying industry, those who benefited from expanding levels of education, and so on—was the subject of the article, and there was in fact an encouraging rise in these people's standard of living. However, the analysis included the bottom group. Simply put, these individuals received no comments.

The writer had been searching for areas of advancement in American society when he came across a very real one. Let me be really honest: I searched for regression and stagnation in this book. Celebrators and chroniclers are overkill for those in American culture who have been rising in the world; they are the stuff of arrogant boasts and claims. But, those who were left behind in the advancement have long since been forgotten.

It is intentional for my perception to be negative and depressing, even if it slightly exaggerates the situation. My moral starting point is anger, the conviction that the clear and pervasive problem of poverty is so appalling that it would be preferable to characterize it in ominous terms rather than downplay it. If the situation is viewed from the most negative angle, nobody will be harmed, but optimism might result in complacency and the continuance of the other America.

It is not intended to imply that the numbers in this book are false or misrepresented. These originate from official government sources, and I have personally verified them in the majority of cases by chatting to residents while roaming the streets of slums or going to the scorching-hot fields where California migrants work. Nonetheless, there is a comprehensible and legal domain where different interpretations and points of view lead to different outcomes.

For instance, the author of Robert Lampman's Senate research states that the estimate of the percentage of low-income persons in the United States might "reasonably vary" between 16 and 36 percent. The variations involved in these criteria might not appear to be very significant when expressed as percentages. Nevertheless, when these numbers are converted to human beings, there is a large and visible difference: the high figure comprises 36,000,000 more people than the low one.

Also, one's perception of the kind of people that constitute the culture of poverty will depend on the figure they choose. Less large families will be included and a higher percentage of the elderly will be included the lower the cutoff line used to define poverty. This is certainly of utmost relevance because at the very least, a study of poverty should direct American attention to the populations that require special assistance.

The statistical presumptions and fundamental interpretations that form the basis for the remainder of the book have been presented. It is unavoidable in such a discussion to become tangled up in technical, impolite, dry topics. The important truth that these figures represent actual people should not be concealed by this, and any tendency toward understatement is an intellectual way of accepting misery.

Two guiding concepts have served as my guide: to provide the data as accurately and objectively as possible; and to speak passionately on behalf of the humanity of those who live in a culture of poverty. It would not be that significant if a statistician discovered a technical error and could demonstrate that there are 10,000,000 fewer poor people. Give or take ten million, the American poor are one of the biggest scandals in a country that has the resources to guarantee every man, woman, and kid a decent life.

Conservatives in England used to argue against change on the basis that the average British worker at the time had a longer life expectancy than a medieval aristocrat. This was in the nineteenth century. This means that defining poverty is, in large part, a function of historical conditioning. In fact, if one wanted to fool around with the numbers, one might show that there aren't many impoverished people in the United States, or at the very least, that their situation isn't as dire as that of the majority of people in Hong Kong. Although famine is a societal issue in American society, it is not as pervasive as it is in other of the newly independent countries. Though few in number, there are still those Americans who literally pass away on the streets.

This conceptualization of poverty that contrasts various eras or societies has very tangible repercussions. It served as a means for the British conservative of the nineteenth century to ignore the plight of employees who were subjected to the most cruel working conditions. If conditions were commonplace in modern society that were similar to those in the English cities a century ago, the conservative of the twenty-first century would be astonished and horrified. Our expectations of what constitutes a decent existence should evolve over time, as they should.

This change has two key components. First, new standards for what a human standard of living ought to be have been established. This has been especially true recently because technology has continuously increased man's potential by making a longer, healthier, and better life possible. Even though they have a better standard of living than Asian peasants or medieval knights, the poor are individuals who experience conditions of existence that are far below what is ideal.

The social notion of poverty is connected to this technological advancement. The impoverished in America are not those in Hong Kong or the sixteenth century; they are those in the country right now. They lack access to what the rest of the country takes for granted and what society could offer if it had the desire. They reside in a marginal area. They consume wealthy America's cinema and magazines, which inform them that they are internal exiles.

Some people might think that defining a definition of poverty is the wrong place for this depiction of the impoverished people's feelings. Yet if this book reveals anything, it's that this feeling of exclusion fuels pessimism and defeatism, which only serves to exacerbate the isolation. Having one bowl of rice in a society when everyone else has half a bowl could be seen as a sign of success and intelligence; it could also inspire someone to act and realize their full potential. In a culture where the majority of people eat a reasonable, balanced diet, it is tragic to consume five bowls of rice.

To define poverty, this statement can be made in a different approach. As a result of our new technology, new needs have been generated. Those who live longer are more prevalent. They therefore require more. In other words, if technology advances without accompanying social progress, there will almost certainly be an increase in human suffering and poverty.

Finally, one must calculate the social cost of progress when defining poverty. The fact that more wives are working now and that family income has increased as a result is one of the reasons why the income statistics indicate fewer persons today with low earnings than twenty years ago. The percentage of working spouses increased from 15% in 1940 to 30% in 1957. So, there must have been greater wealth and less poverty.

Yet a large surge in the number of working women is an expensive way to improve income. It will be paid for by the depreciation of home life and the deprivation of children's care, love, and supervision. For instance, this particular truth may very well have a big impact on the issues facing young people in America. It can imply that some or all of the following generation will be responsible for footing the cost for the extra money made. It could imply that while income figures have improved, thousands or even hundreds of thousands of children have suffered as a result. Who is to claim that someone is no longer impoverished if they have more money but acquired it by mortgaging their future?

It is challenging to put all these ambiguities together and define poverty in the United States in a straightforward manner. But, the following analysis should clarify some of the underlying presumptions of the claims in this book:

Those who are denied the bare minimum levels of education, housing, food, and health that our current state of scientific knowledge specifies as necessary for life as it is currently lived in the United States should be considered to be in poverty.

A psychological definition of poverty should focus on people who are psychological exiles inside the community, who unavoidably adopt negative attitudes such as defeatism and pessimism, and who are thus unable to take advantage of new opportunities.

It is essential to define poverty in terms of what it might mean for people and society as a whole. America as a whole suffers as long as the country falls short of its potential. We are all poorer as a result of what others experience.

The most straightforward method to estimate the number of poor individuals in the United States is to use the income figures provided by various government agencies. Without question, this technique overlooks numerous small distinctions. For instance, it does not accommodate individual variation: How good a cook is a certain wife? What are the typical dishes of a certain ethnic group and what are their prices? This approach minimizes the significance of the growing number of working wives. The income test does, however, offer a rough indicator of poverty in the United States, although missing the quality of life in the other America.

The poverty level for an urban family of four was set at $2,000 by low-income studies conducted by special congressional committees in the late 1940s. It would be roughly $2,500 per year if this were brought up to date (i.e., if it were simply adjusted for inflationary adjustments that have occurred in the intervening years). Nonetheless, a number of experts contended that the definition's low minimum income level at the time the number was determined. Also, this test implicitly presupposes that there shouldn't be any advancement over the period of a decade by just updating it to reflect prices from 1961. In other words, it ignores the reality that other groups in society advanced throughout this time.

A recent study by Robert Lampman established the low-income threshold for a family of four living in an urban area using a $2,500 cutoff. Lampman then made the assumption that other family sizes would be directly proportional to this amount; a person living in an urban area would be considered low income if he received $1,157; a family of six would be considered low income if its yearly income take was $3,236; and so on. Based on this, Lampman calculated that 32,000,000 Americans, or 19% of the country's population, fell into the low-income category.

The AFL-CIO employed a marginally stricter definition of what constituted low income over the same time period. It was discovered that 36,000,000 Americans had household sizes of two or more and had 1958 incomes of less $3,000 per year. 5,500,000 more people were surviving on less than $1,500 per year, or less than $29 per week before taxes. The AFL-CIO statistics would contend that 41,500,000 Americans, or 24% of the population, had clearly below-average incomes.

The Bureau of Labor Statistics has released a report since the Lampman and AFL-CIO estimations, which would suggest that both of these studies tended to underestimate the issue. Lampman assumed throughout his study that a four-person urban family's "sufficient" budget, in terms of the Bureau of Labor Statistics, would be just over $4,000 per year. The same amount was estimated to be $4,800 annually by the AFL-CIO.

Yet, the foundation for both of these estimates was a definition of "adequacy" created by the government in the late 1940s (and adjusted, without changing the basic concepts, for price increases over the intervening years). The Department of Labor Statistics just released a revised budget for a four-person urban family. The range is $5,370 in Houston to $6,567 in Chicago, with $6,147 about being the national average in Washington, D.C. These numbers, in the government's estimation, indicate a budget that is significantly over "basic maintenance" and somewhat below "luxury." It is described as "minimal but adequate," yet it is "below the average experienced by American families."

Before attempting to define poverty, it is vital to briefly discuss this budget because it is a significant attempt to characterize income needs. According to these government statistics, a family of four consists of an employed 38-year-old husband, a wife who does not have a job outside the home, an 8-year-old girl, and a 13-year-old son. The family resides in the suburbs or a big city in a rented home. The budget was created using fall 1959 prices.

As they were calculated in Washington, D.C. (the city closest to the national average), some representative examples of the budget items are provided below: With $1,447 spent on meals at home and $181 on eating out, the total budget for food came to $1,684; the rent came to $1,226; and the wife had $160 to spend on apparel for the year. Obviously, this is hardly a budget for the opulent lifestyle shown in American periodicals. In modern words, it is not poverty or anything resembling it. Yet, if the family head were to experience a severe illness or long-term unemployment, the family would be in a significant crisis.

The method used by the Bureau of Labor Statistics to determine the cost of keeping families smaller or bigger than the normal example of four is a crucial component of its budget. For instance, the budget for two people is somewhat higher than 60% of the budget for a family of four.

On this basis, if the cutoff were established somewhere between $3,000 and $3,500 for an urban family of four, if one were to take approximately half of this budget as the standard for low income or poverty (making all the adjustments for smaller families, for low income individuals, for lower costs, and for food grown in farm areas), then the culture of poverty would be roughly defined in the United States as composed of around 50,000,000 people. That would be more than 60,000,000 if using Lampman's estimates and using $4,000 as the cut-off, which is the highest level he deems to be a "realistic" estimate of low income.

It serves no purpose to engage in an interminable methodological debate over the precise threshold of family poverty.

Lampman's figure of 32,000,000 poor people can be viewed as a minimum definition; the AFL-CIO figure of 41,000,000 would be a very reasonable definition; and, given the revisions made by the Bureau of Labor Statistics, the total of 50,000,000 poor Americans would reflect our most recent statement of living standards.

In other words, between 20 and 25 percent of Americans live in poverty. Their housing, healthcare, food, and opportunities are subpar. They number between 40,000,000 and 50,000,000 people in my opinion.

Nonetheless, it's crucial to avoid being overly careful. These numbers may need to be revised higher in the future. The way that the number of low-income people varies depending on a recession or prosperous condition is one of the most noticeable aspects of the Department of Commerce statistics. For instance, Commerce reported in 1947 that 34% of family units had an annual income of less than $3,000 (in 1961 currency). This increased to 36% of the families with incomes under $3,000 in 1961, which was 1949, a recessionary year. 1950, a year of restored prosperity, saw a decrease in this percentage to 33% of the total. The 1950s were marked by this pattern.

The conditions of a particular time and location are expressed by these percentages and statistics, thus it is important to recognize this while using them. In this instance, they speak of a period of recent affluence and a modest recession. (The latest figures, 1961, are from the late 1950s.) The future trajectory of the United States' overall economic situation will influence the data on poverty in some way. The other Americans tend to be progress-immune, so they do not automatically partake in the profits of good times, but they do automatically share in the losses of bad ones. Millions of people barely make it out of poverty. All the data in this chapter would need to be revised upward in the event of stagnation, a recession, or even a persistently high unemployment rate during a period of prosperity.

Most of our study has thus far been focused on an effort to establish a minimal standard for existence in American society and to estimate the number of people who fall below this line. If one moves on to a similar question— How has the general-distribution pattern of income been evolving in the United States?—the conclusions are even more striking. The following table provides a very clear explanation of what has been taking place. (It was obtained from Department of Commerce data and is taken from an AFL-CIO pamphlet.)

How Total Family Income Was Shared Before Taxes
1935–36, 1944, and 1958

Families by fifths	1935–36 (Percent)	1944 (Percent)	1958 (Percent)	Average income per family, 1958
Lowest	4.1%	4.9%	4.7%	$1,460
2nd	9.2	10.9	11.1	3,480
3rd	14.1	16.2	16.3	5,110
4th	20.9	22.2	22.4	7,020
Highest	51.7	45.8	45.5	14,250

How are these percentages to be interpreted? The United States' lowest fifth of families had 4.7 percent of the nation's total personal income in 1958, while the highest fifth, which included the wealthiest families, had 45.5 percent. The trend in

American income distribution during this time is more significant than this astounding comparison. The poor (those who reside in the lowest fifth of society and beyond) had an increase in their proportion of personal income from 4.1 percent to 4.9 percent between 1935–1936 and 1944. The relative situation of the most vulnerable Americans was improving in a sluggish, tortoise-like manner. The postwar era, however, saw a reversal of this trend. In 1958 the poor had less of a share of personal income than they did in 1944.

In fact, this graph is one of the statistical explanations for why poverty in America is so invisible. The third, fourth, and top groups are those that include college graduates, politically engaged individuals, authors and editors, etc. The middle level has seen consistent advancement, and things are generally looking up and moving forward. There was a drop at the very peak, but it needs to be understood in its wider context. The neediest fifth of Americans saw an average real income increase of $80 between 1944 and 1958, while the richest 5 percent (with average 1958 incomes of $25,280) saw an increase of $1,900. In conclusion, the experience hasn't exactly been terrible, despite the fact that the percentages at the very top show a slight reduction (although, as will be seen, it is doubtful whether this is the reality).

If these numbers are startling, a further exclusion must be made to magnify their impact. Nearly all of these income numbers are based on official reports, which often overstate the wealth of the wealthy. There is no malice in stating this fact. It is merely a consequence of the capacity of high-income families and individuals to hide income in order to avoid paying income taxes. This can be accomplished by using extravagant expense accounts (which are included in a standard of living but excluded from income numbers), through stock transactions that are not taken into account in the computations for commerce.

Some people might be surprised to find that taxes typically harm the poor. According to a 1960 Tax Foundation research, families earning under $2,000 pay 28.3 percent of their income to the federal, state, and local governments, while families earning between five and seven times as much only pay 24 percent of their income to the government. (This is due in part to the state and local governments' significant usage of property and excise taxes. They take a considerably larger percentage from the poor because they are distributed "equitably" to everyone.)

Hence, to put it mildly, and without accounting for the widespread underreporting at high income levels, the poor in American society today are in a worse relative situation than they were 15 years ago. Their proportion of prosperity has diminished as technology has grown, while their involvement in recession and misery has increased.

The identity of the major groups has already been well established. The elderly, minorities, farm workers, and industrial rejects are the main subcultures of poverty.

What percentage of these individuals live in the world of the poor?

There are two basic ways in our contemporary narrative to explain away the significance of poverty in American culture.

On the one hand, there is the idea that there are "pockets" of poverty, which has already been discussed. But, there is a rather peculiar theory. The impoverished are rural and non-White, it claims. This is regrettable, to be sure, but it indicates that poverty is a problem that only affects a small portion of the country, that it is linked to underdeveloped regions, and that it will surely be eliminated by developing technology. (I've been told that it was formerly common practice in Australia to produce income and standard-of-living statistics by leaving out the aborigines. In this nation, the rural poor and Black people frequently receive the same treatment.)

But the idea that rural and non-white people are disproportionately poor in America is at odds with the reality.

Robert Lampman's analysis gives a conservative estimate of the total number of low-income people at 32,000,000. As Lampman himself points out, one of the effects of his definition is that it removes a significant number of large family units that are located just on the other side of his cutoff line. Lampman's work is excellent, even with his low estimate for what constitutes poverty and this one misconception that results from it.

helps in figuring out how many people from different groups live in a culture of poverty.

Of Lampman's 32,000,000 poor population, 8,000,000 people were 65 years of age or older, 6,400,000 people were non-White, 8,000,000 lived in consumer units led by women, and 21,000,000 lived in units headed by people with at least an eighth-grade education. The fact that poverty tends to cluster misery is one of the most significant single truths about it, hence it is obvious that these numbers overlap.

According to Lampman's research, one or more of the traits that likely to make a person fall behind were present in 70% of the low-income population. 50 percent of the general population has one or more of these impairments. So, it is customary to encounter someone who is the victim of a series of setbacks: a Negro who lives in a family unit headed by a woman, faces work discrimination, has less advanced educational training, and is a member of a racial minority.

Age is one of the limitations mentioned by Lampman. Yet in this case, some terminology clarification is required. According to statistics, "age" is now seen as starting at 65 in America. However, the actual cutoff under these circumstances is much younger, as is made evident in the chapter on relocated workers and depressed areas. The economic definition of old age in the workplace is between the ages of forty and fifty. If a worker between these ages is laid off, his chances of finding a new job at his previous level of pay are reduced, regardless of his skill. If he is an unskilled or semiskilled worker (or if his skill has been rendered obsolete by technology), the odds are against him ever finding a comparable job.

This is an illustration of how biological facts are interpreted in relation to societal norms. Because of the awful psychological experience of rejection and defeat, discrimination against blue-collar workers 40 years of age or older also exists in practice. It may be required to change the entire notion of what defines aging in America if, as seems to be the case, this problem worsens in the near future.

Lampman comes to a very significant conclusion at the other end of the age spectrum: children make up a larger proportion of the culture of poverty than do the elderly. There are 8,000,000 people over the age of 65 and 11,000,000 children under the age of 18 in his 32,000,000 low-income population. Hence, the young make up one-third of the population. This fact is really important. As was mentioned in a previous chapter, a significant number of the elderly fall into poverty after working lives with a respectable level of living. There is a certain type of tragedy that the country has created by allowing life to increase without providing for its proper maintenance. Nevertheless, there is another bleak process at work with poor children: it's possible that they will become the parents of the subsequent generation of the poor culture.

Many younger people are beginning their lives in a state of inherited poverty, as Lampman observes. As I have argued elsewhere in this book, at the moment this fact may be more important than at any other period in the country's history. The character of poverty has altered, and it has become more fatal for the young. It is no longer connected to immigrant groups with great expectations; rather, it now stands for people whose social circumstances make it more and harder for them to integrate into society at large. The economy's educational requirements are rising at the same time.

The vast majority of these underprivileged kids attend the worst schools. Even when they have educational chances, they come from families who have a low opinion of education and who advocate the earliest possible legal leave-taking from school.

Hence, the country is starting the 1960s with a very grave issue: a huge concentration of youth who, if they do not receive urgent assistance, may very possibly be the cause of a type of hereditary poverty that is new to American society. If this theory is accurate, the culture of poverty's vicious cycle is, if anything, intensifying, getting more disabling, and becoming a concern because it is becoming more and more associated with the accident of birth.

In any event, poverty in the United States is neither a problem exclusive to people of color nor restricted to rural areas. About 25% of other America is made up of non-White people, which is double the national average. Rural poor people make up even less of the total population (and there is overlap, because poor Negroes in the countryside are an important grouping). The theory, which somehow takes solace in the notion of "marginal" poverty, cannot be supported by the evidence.

The unique health tragedies that affect the elderly were described in an earlier chapter. But, it's crucial to recognize that disease is a general impairment that affects everyone in the culture of poverty, regardless of age. I first noticed this during the Asian-flu outbreak in New York in the fifties. The newspapers said that the outbreak was socially class-based; therefore, poorer districts experienced considerably lower rates of the disease than densely populated places like Harlem and the Lower East Side.

Here are just a few figures from the US National Health Survey on the physical abuse that the impoverished in America experience:

Children in families with incomes of $4,000 or more had a rate of dental visits that was three times higher than that of children in families with lower incomes for the age range of five to fourteen.

The rate of tooth loss among Americans is closely correlated with family income; the less money a family makes, the more likely it is that all of its teeth will be lost.

The proportion of people who have activity or mobility restrictions is directly correlated with income across all age groups; between the ages of forty-five and sixty-four, families with incomes under $2,000 have six times more mobility restrictions than those with incomes of $7,000 or more.

As a result, families with earnings under $2,000 suffered 32.4 restricted-activity days per person per year, which is more restricted activity days than any other group in society. The matching number for families earning between $2,000 and $3,999 was 20.5 days of restricted activity per person, and for families earning $4,000 or more, it was almost 16.5 days.

The final quote comes from an assessment of conditions between July 1957 and June 1958 by the National Health Survey. The analysis adds, "A plausible reason for this link is that persons in lower-income families are more susceptible to limiting sickness due of less use of medical care, poorer food, and other variables," after stating these data.

The reality of health insurance does not give any reason to believe that this scenario will improve any time soon. From July to December 1959 was the time frame covered by the National Health Survey. In spite of making up 15% of the population at the time, people with incomes under $1,999 only received 7.4% of hospital insurance, 6.6 percent of surgical insurance, and 7.0 percent of doctor visit insurance. Contrarily, while making up 35.6% of the population, the $4,000–$6,999 income bracket has 42.1 percent of all hospital insurance, 43.1 percent of all surgery insurance, and 40.6 percent of all doctor visit insurance.

Thirdly, geography is a significant factor in the culture of poverty. In 1959, 16 percent of families with earnings under $3,000 lived in the Northeast, 16 percent in the West, 21 percent did so in the North Central region, and 34 percent did so in the South, according to data from the Department of Commerce. The significant advancement between 1953 and 1959 was in the West, the proportion of families with incomes under $3,000 decreased from 23 percent to 16 percent.

The region that made the least progress was the North Central, where the percentage of poverty families decreased by just 1% during a six-year period.

When reading these numbers (or any statistics pertaining to families), it is important to keep in mind that "unattached persons" who are poor are far more likely to reside in urban areas and be disconnected from rural life. This would lessen the scandal that the South's relative situation is when measured by the standard of family poverty. There are 5,500,000 "single person families" with an annual income of less than $1,500, according to AFL-CIO estimates. This does not include the nearly 250,000 elderly institutional population.)

In conclusion, a brief statistical portrait of the alternate America can be created.

In America, the percentage of the impoverished in the population is around 25%. Depending on the definition of low income used, they range in number from 40,000,000 to 50,000,000.

Although non-white minorities experience the most severe and concentrated poverty of any group, the bulk of the impoverished in America are white.

Although rural poverty is one of the most significant aspects of the culture of poverty, it does not constitute its mass base. Both the number and percentage of the poor who work on farms is dropping.

In addition to non-white minorities, other disadvantaged groups include the elderly, migrant workers, industrial rejects, children, families with a female head of household, and those with low levels of education. These numerous aspects of the poverty culture frequently co-occur. There are more children among the poor since large families have experienced the least growth of any family type in recent years.

The people who are in this situation are at a severe physical disadvantage, suffer from more chronic illnesses, and have fewer therapeutic options.

More mental and emotional issues are experienced by people who live in a culture of poverty than by any other group in American society.

None of the complacent theories—that poverty is now concentrated in certain "pockets," that it is nonwhite and rural, etc.—are supported by these data. Instead, they point to a big issue that is really dangerous because it affects those who have become immune to change and who have an upside-down perspective on technological advancement.

This chapter would end as it did at the beginning. These are the numbers, and genuine men have a right to debate the specifics and argue that one interpretation is either too high or too low. I would implore the reader to put the number game out of their minds at this point. Despite the exact measurements, it is clear that the figures reflect a huge, intolerably high level of human misery in this country. They ought to be read with outrage in mind.

A poor America will continue to exist, a horrible example of needless suffering in the most developed civilization in the world, until these facts embarrass us and prompt us to take action.

POVERTY IN THE 1970s

Congress agreed when Lyndon B. Johnson announced a "unconditional war" on poverty in 1964, and throughout the following four years, the White House cited impressive figures about the billions being spent on social causes. The 1960s saw a rise in activism, student and church commitments to end hunger, as well as widespread media coverage of the domestic embarrassment of the country through documentaries. In fact, there was such a perception of frantic government activity that Richard Nixon ran for president in 1968 on a platform of slowing the pace of innovation. How would one then make the case that poverty would continue in the 1970s and possibly reappear in society's conscience and consciousness?

The government has, as usual, carefully gathered the data to refute the optimism of the previous administration and the reticence of the current administration. The United States only gives its least fortunate residents a small portion of what they badly need in every important area, including food, shelter, education, and other social duties. Without intervention, the offspring of this generation's poverty will raise an even greater generation in the other America because half of the poor are young people who will enter a sophisticated economy at a significant disadvantage.

This is not to suggest that advancements have not been made. The boom brought on by government policies in the 1960s did eventually lower unemployment rates, and some people saw genuine but illusory advantages as a result. And even though inflation tainted some of its impact, Medicare for the Elderly was the only program where social investment experienced something akin to a quantum leap.

Even so, the same demographics that were impoverished in 1962, when this book was first published, remain so today: black people, Spanish-speaking people, the unemployed and underemployed, residents of economically devastated areas, the aging. And I should also include one minority group that I erroneously left out of my initial analysis: American Indians, who are arguably the poorest of all.

The society has nevertheless begun to celebrate paper victories over poverty, despite the fact that it has failed to fulfill its promises from the 1960s. As a result, the Department of Commerce joyfully reported in August 1969 that in just nine years, the number of people living in poverty had decreased from 39,000,000 to 25,000,000. The figures simply prettied up reality, which is the main issue, as will be evident. This suggested that America might be returning to the established practices of the Eisenhower years in the 1970s, deluding itself with optimistic pronouncements about the state of the country. Another alarming sign came when Arthur Burns, one of Richard Nixon's top domestic advisers, claimed that poverty is just a "intellectual construct" determined by "fabricated statistics" in the summer of 1969. That particular brand of callous thinking is what initially rendered the poor invisible. And it might occur once more.

So, it is vital to look past the current optimism with its juggling of the social books in order to comprehend the harsh possibilities for poverty in the 1970s. Since modern society, in one of its many ironies, has spared no expense in documenting its injustices, it is far simpler to accomplish that now than it was in the early 1960s. The challenge is to critically analyze official statistics in order to see the human faces and tragic tendencies that are concealed within. Then, we'll be able to estimate how much work is still left to complete.

Many people believe that statistics are an impartial, scientific depiction of the real world in an economy that is overflowing with data. The estimates are actually based on questionable and highly politicized hypotheses, which explains how poverty can continue even as some government organizations are ready to celebrate its extinction.

There wasn't much study available when Lyndon Johnson announced his social war in the 1964 State of the Union address. Robert Lampman, a committed academic who had exposed the illusion of universal prosperity in the 1950s, had carried out a large portion of it. Citing his research, the Council of Economic Advisers declared in 1964 that a family's annual income of less than $3,000 qualified as being in poverty. Even though it was only an approximate estimate because it didn't account for family size or geography, it was quite helpful in pinpointing the groups that were most affected.

The criteria were greatly improved throughout the course of the following few years. The Social Security Administration made a remarkable effort to define poverty objectively by using the Department of Agriculture's Economic Food Plan as a starting point. This was almost 80% of the Low Cost Plan, which many welfare organizations had previously utilized.

It was an emergency diet that was only meant to be brief. In January 1964, the "line" was $3,100, and the Economy Plan offered $4.60 per person per week, or 22 cents per meal. A four-person household was considered poor in 1967 if its income was less than $3,335 per year, or $4.90 per week. The poverty threshold was raised all the way to $3,553 per year in 1969, when the Department of Commerce was releasing its happy news.

These definitions were created by concerned government employees, some of whom had a strong personal motivation to put an end to the outrage they were defining. Even though the poverty threshold was raised in 1968 to reflect changes in the cost of living as measured by the Consumer Price Index, it was still far too low. For starters, organized social groupings like unions and middle-class professionals and technicians constantly attempt to raise their yearly incomes by more than the rate of inflation. As a result, it is believed that everyone's absolute standard of living should rise annually. But, the statisticians are effectively arguing that the poor should never advance as a category by just revising the poverty criterion for price increases. Second, the late 1960s inflationary increases were particularly severe in the field of medical services, practically canceling out the increase in Medicare, and some persons were forced out of Medicaid.

Before there is excessive celebration over the paper victories in the fight against poverty, it would be wise to examine read the President's Commission on Income Maintenance Programs' 1969 report. The nation was informed that the official definition should be expanded by more than half (from $2.43 per person per day to $4.05), according to a Department of Labor research.

But far more telling was the commission's observation that between 1965 and 1966, 36% of families managed to escape poverty, whereas 34% did so. That highlighted how dangerous life was for those who had managed to scramble above the line; it implied that millions were being forced into the other America even in the midst of a boom and a "war" on poverty.

There was also another optimistic assumption in the official definition. Assuming that all other necessities would cost twice as much as food, the Economy Food Plan was used as the starting point. According to Herman Miller of the Bureau of the Census, this connection between food and income was discovered in 1955. So, one should compute the other products at three times the price of food, not two, to keep up with developments in the economy and society since that time. Miller came to the conclusion that the government eliminated the poverty of the twelve million Americans who were still living in poverty by applying the tenets of the Eisenhower Fifty.

Consider the infamous census undercount in 1960 if it sounds outrageous to believe that sincere, and even caring, specialists could thus ignore the suffering of twelve million of their fellow citizens. Over six million Americans were not even included, the majority of whom were black adults residing in northern cities. Without a regular employment, a fixed location, access to the mail, or a phone number, their lives were so minimal that they were not even afforded the dignity of being a statistic. Once again, the degree of suffering was grossly overestimated, but this time the mistake has been made public.

So, it is not just the poor who suffer when officialdom adopts an overly sanguine attitude. Undoubtedly, they live in a subculture of particular indignities where institutions like the family, the police, and the schools act differently than they do in the rest of society. But, they are also a part of society as a whole, and when they are disregarded, so are countless numbers of people who are not in poverty. Ironically, the white worker who was tempted to vote for George Wallace in 1968 because he was fed up with the government helping the poor and minorities "too much" will suffer if the programs are reduced.

Because the Council of Economic Advisers defined twelve million Americans as "near poor" in 1967 (defined as having an annual income for a family of four between $3,335 and $4,345). Sixteen million Americans are just one disease, one accident, or one recession away from becoming poor once again if these figures were underestimated in the same manner that poverty itself was. This group will suffer almost as much loss as the impoverished if America in the 1970s scales back its social activities, which now seems so likely.

Nevertheless, there is another, far larger group of people whose fate is connected to that of the other Americans without their knowledge. The Bureau of Labor Statistics estimated that it would cost $9,191 for an urban family of four to maintain a "moderate standard of living" in late 1966, which is light-years away from the 1970s in terms of inflation. With that amount, you could purchase a two-year-old used car and a new suit every four years. Moreover, the majority of Americans had less. For housing, food, and education, they had to work hard. Turning our backs on the impoverished poor produces a political and social environment in which the demands of the majority can be disregarded, just as raising the minimum wage for the lowest paid workers tends to assist raise the take of those who are organized and considerably better wealthy.

Hence, there will be more poor people in the 1970s than is shown by official statistics. But maybe the simplest way to understand the perilous trends is to look at one generation's worth of unfulfilled housing promises to realize that the 1970s will probably be another unsuccessful decade.

In 1949, the government pledged to provide each resident with a good home. The Congress came to the conclusion that the private housing market was failing to meet the requirements of the underprivileged under the leadership of a conservative Republican, Senator Robert A. Taft. As a result, they committed to constructing 810,000 low-cost housing units by 1955. One generation later, in 1970, that goal has still not been met. But, the issue was not just with what the government did not do, but also with what it did. Washington was depriving the poor of housing while giving more than ten million wealthy home builders in suburbia access to low-cost financing and opulent tax benefits. "Government action through urban renewal, highway programs, demolition on public housing sites, code enforcement, and other programs has destroyed more housing for the poor than government at all levels has built for them," the President's Commission on Urban Problems, presided over by Senator Paul Douglas, reported in January 1969.

As a result, a legislation was created in 1968 solemnly committing the US to uphold its commitments made in the 1950s in the 1970s. But within a year, it became obvious that the country's ability to fulfill this second, shamefaced pledge was improbable. Increasing the production of housing for the poor to twenty times the current rate would be necessary to create twenty-six million additional housing units in ten years, six million of them at low cost. Yet as Secretary of Housing and Urban Development George Romney said in 1969, it's entirely likely that we'll fall 10 million units short of the stated objective. What this portends for the 1970s is that American center cities will continue to deteriorate, the housing poverty rate—which now affects a third of the population—will rise, and ghost towns will start to appear in the midst of major cities.

For the plight of the cities is getting so painful that even slums are not as profitable as they used to be. As a result, between ten and fifteen thousand properties are abandoned annually, according to the Real Estate Research Corporation, which reported this to the Wall Street Journal in 1969. For instance, I was raised in a part of St. Louis, Missouri, where my grandfather used to dwell. It was inhabited by white middle class individuals and had large three-story homes with roomy lawns and backyards. After 25 years, going back to the same neighborhood was like going into a combat zone. Some of the houses were boarded up and vacant while others were in disrepair. That avenue was actually passing away.

Many Americans would drive down that block and believe it to be evidence that the underprivileged don't value property and will demolish any decent house they come across.

They were stupid enough to accept one. That is wholly untrue in every way. That street and the thousands of others like it in America's major cities are the result of a generation of broken promises, as well as major economic trends like job loss and inflation, which served to isolate and imprison the poor, both black and white, in the run-down pass-down homes of the white middle class that had relocated to the suburbs using federal subsidies.

As the country marked its 200th birthday on July 4, 1976, there were likely more ghost villages in the metropolis.

But, the numbers fail to capture the sentimental atmosphere of the 1960s, when expectations were sky-high before being crushed. A few personal examples might help.

John Kennedy started a war on poverty within the government, but he was unable to declare it in public. Lyndon Johnson declared it in January 1964. Sargent Shriver was appointed to lead the effort in February. I traveled to Washington to have lunch with Shriver and ended up staying for two weeks as a member of a task force that toiled feverishly for sixteen to eighteen hours each day to try to establish the project's fundamental ideas.

It wasn't just crucial that the president would donate money to the fight against poverty. However, this project benefited from the huge moral and political power that the White House can muster. The metropolis was buzzing with enthusiasm and social passion. Friends of mine who work for the government called to say they would join this cause even at a lower level and pay. After those exhausting fourteen days, Frank Mankiewicz, Paul Jacobs, and I wrote a memo to Shriver stating that if the task was going to get done, dramatic ideas that went beyond the New Deal were required. In his first speech at the White House,

Shriver included some of our research, and he told us that Mr. Johnson was unfazed by the issue's extreme characterization.

A rally was held on the University of California Berkeley campus a few weeks later. When I spoke about the Johnson program to a big group of students, they were excited. These were the same young people who, within two or three years, would vehemently disagree with the president and aid in his ouster from politics in 1968. And exactly because they had put their faith in the promises made in 1964, this would be one of the factors contributing to their furious disenchantment.

When running for president in 1964, the Teamsters Union in Los Angeles held a strike meeting. The leadership made the unusual decision to schedule an educational session prior to the business session since they were aware that strike and contract ratification votes always draw quite a sizable crowd. I explained to a packed room of white employees that it was in their financial best interest to join forces with the poor and the disadvantaged in order to build a truly full-employment economy. And there was vociferous, resounding support for that viewpoint.

The Economic Opportunity Act's Community Action measures then started to work in favorably. As Daniel Patrick Moynihan has argued, there was a lot of misunderstanding regarding what the phrase "maximum feasible participation" of the poor meant in the fight against poverty; mayors wanted to give the poor more favors and wanted them to be "deserving"; sociologists and psychologists saw a chance to test theories. Yet, despite the fact that almost as soon as it was revealed, the administration started to back away from the idea of democratic involvement, the activists of the other America seized the opportunity.

A protest took place in Oxnard, California, in March 1965. The parade worked its way through the Mexican American neighborhood of town, led by a mariachi band and a man riding a horse. This was an early example of the movement César Chávez created among migrant farmworkers, including Filipino, Anglo, and Mexican American workers. For the first time in a generation, Chávez had boosted the hopes of the men and women who gather the grapes of wrath with the strong backing of the existing unions, assistance from students, and support from religious individuals.

An emerging rebellion was the Oxnard farmworkers' union. Another protest in Montgomery, Alabama, that same month served as the finale of a much older conflict. Tens of thousands of people from all around the nation joined the Selma marchers as they made their way to Montgomery, led by Martin Luther King Jr. We passed through dark slums on our way to the capital. The overwhelming display of unity left the people seated on the dilapidated porches confused. Some joined the line of march, while others gaped in shock and even sobbed. The Voting Rights Act of 1965 was ultimately won by the African-American community with the help of their friends, who included trade unionists, clergy, ministers, rabbis, nuns, liberal and radical political figures.

Confederate flags were flying everywhere as we stood in front of the capitol. The "Star-Spangled Banner" then abruptly changed into a song of militant hope that the country could unite as the audience chanted it defiantly. Additionally, a majority of the electorate would have been represented by the forces present in Montgomery had they remained together. Nevertheless, they didn't. Due to this

In the midst of his victory, President Johnson was planning to escalate the Vietnam War. The anti-poverty initiatives persisted, and the language remained forceful. Yet, tens of billions of dollars and Washington's moral and political resources were diverted from the right domestic struggle to the incorrect war in Southeast Asia.

The most militant among the black poor were angry and disillusioned, turning against the entire system. The majority of the idealistic students joined the Robert Kennedy and Eugene McCarthy campaigns in 1968 and helped to force the president out of the race, while a minority were pushed into an ineffectual but noisy intransigence. The unionists continued to back Johnson's war policy while also remaining dedicated to fighting poverty. They are the group that brings the most political clout to the legislative endeavor. As a result, the allies who had stood side by side that March afternoon in Montgomery turned against one another as Vietnam came to gradually dominate all aspects of American life.

The funerals of 1968.

The Poor People's Movement, which aimed to create an economic bill of rights for all Americans, was underway when Martin Luther King Jr. passed away. The organizations that had gathered in Montgomery—the blacks, the unionists, the liberals and radicals from the middle class, and the churches—met in Memphis the day before he was buried. Because King was working with sanitation workers who were on strike and campaigning for union recognition when he was killed. We then marched through a nearly deserted downtown in the name of the deceased leader. Memphis residents had chosen to stay at home that day, so the only sound in the city's core was the unsettling patter of feet. Federalized guardsmen were stationed in groups along the side streets to defend our constitutional rights.

Ironically, rioting and tension were caused by the passing of the greatest proponent of nonviolence in America. That was how acrid the conflict had grown.

Then, in June 1968, Robert Kennedy passed away. The citizens of the alternate America felt as though fate was robbing them of the leaders that cared about and battled for them. I had backed Kennedy because I thought he had a special ability to communicate with both black and white poor people as well as white trade unionists. I participated in a speech alongside César Chávez and John Lewis, the leader of the Student Nonviolent Coordinating Committee in its early, nonviolent days, at a meeting in California during the primary that served as a symbol of that hope. Nevertheless, a murderer put a stop to that movement's dream in June.

This would appeal to Latinos, unionists, middle-class idealists, and people of color.

Together with the senator's body, that funeral train seemed to me to be carrying the best hopes of the decade. Because the wealthy seldom live within earshot of the tracks, while the impoverished do, it went through the other America. These tens of thousands of people were mourning their own goals with the guy who had spoken for them while occasionally singing, saluting, or just being there and silent. Because of the catastrophe in Vietnam, the 1960s saw the greatest chance for social reform since the New Deal. And the disillusionment and memories of these awful deaths will be passed on to the 1970s.

Richard Nixon was elected president and declared that the federal government had tried to accomplish too much and that he would thus decentralize social programs and set more modest goals after all the broken promises and failed starts. His analysis contained a hazardous untruth and a half-truth, which is bad news for the underprivileged in the 1970s.

The administration under Lyndon Johnson had in fact made it seem as though it were pulling off extraordinary feats. They believed that Washington had done a lot for the poor, especially the Black poor, which is one of the reasons why a startling number of white workers moved toward George Wallace in 1968 (even though, outside the South, they eventually voted for Hubert Humphrey). They mistook the brash language for action and failed to see how little life had changed in the ghettos. As far as Nixon criticizes Johnson for speaking too loudly, he is correct. Nevertheless, the rest of his argument—that the federal government was acting too actively and that its efforts should be scaled back and given to the states—is utterly false.

One only needs to look at a few of the official numbers to dispel the illusion of the favored, pampered poor. The National Commission on Civil Disorders, also known as the "Riot" Commission, reported in 1968 that the median percentage of people who were eligible who were actually covered by any one of the major social programs was 33 percent in Detroit, New Haven, and Newark, the cities where the violence was the most destructive in 1967. In other words, the majority of the poor in the United States do not get any form of welfare. The Commission also demonstrated that, on average, welfare payments are "a little more than half of need" and, in certain situations, only cover one-fourth of need. A special Cabinet committee informed Lyndon Johnson in January 1969 that the current domestic initiatives were already $6 billion underfunded, and that by 1972, a moderate increase of civilian operations in the directions already recommended by numerous commissions and study groups would cost an additional $40 billion.

The numbers so show that the government is slipping billions of dollars behind conservative estimates of what needs to be done. Millions of people must make do with half or a fourth of their urgent requirements among the small percentage of the poor who are fortunate enough to receive any money. Furthermore, the opinions of others who are not impoverished frequently harm these people. Those who receive welfare are viewed by many residents as a burden on the hardworking common man. But, as Richard Titmus has shown, the reality is that a large portion of the poor are receiving insufficient compensation for the humiliations that either the government or the economy, or both, have inflicted upon them.

The rural poor who were pushed into the metropolis in recent years are the most extreme example. Federal subsidies of billions of dollars were given to wealthy people and corporate farms, including Senator James O. Eastland, the unbiased plantation owner who serves on the Senate Agriculture Committee and determines his own compensation, who received hundreds of thousands of dollars. These princely welfare payments to the wealthy allowed them to earn a profit by reducing the land under cultivation and also provided them with funding for mechanization. So it was that production in the fields increased twice as rapidly as in the industry, and millions of the rural poor became economically unnecessary.

Hence, federal funds helped drive 5.5 million black farmworkers into the cities between 1950 and 1966. They were forced to adapt to a confusing, complex urban environment and compete in an advanced job market because they were from communities where education for Black people was of poor quality. As Harold Fleming once put it, they carried "the highest pile of social disadvantages ever visited upon an identifiable community" with them. The fact that the federal government paid billions to the agricultural rich in a way that drove the poor off the land was the underlying cause of the issue, even if these folks frequently appear to the typical taxpayer to be a burden. In other words, the majority of those on welfare lists are a result of government initiatives and advancements in technology. They only get a small portion of the justice-based compensation they are due.

Simply put, Washington has done too much of the wrong things rather than too much of the right things. The main argument of Mr. Nixon's welfare message from 1969 was that "a third of a century of concentrating power in Washington has developed a bureaucratic behemoth, unwieldy, unresponsive, and ineffectual."

merely is not a true account of what transpired. Furthermore, Mr. Nixon's main welfare proposal, which calls for federalizing welfare benefits at a specific level, violates his own research by proposing to set a minimum income for families. Mr. Nixon was appropriately upset that whereas New York has significantly higher requirements, Mississippi pays an average of $39.35 per month to maintain an entire family. In order to stop Mississippi from abusing its states' rights in such a cruel manner, he wants to employ the federal government, which is hardly decentralization.

Hence, the president, who will establish policy guidelines for at least the first half of the 1970s, has a flimsy, incoherent understanding of poverty. And some of the issues he will encounter will be far as severe than those that Lyndon Johnson dealt with.

The fact that almost half of the poor population is young is among the most alarming statistics concerning them. The Department of Labor anticipates that there will be 50% more black teenagers and 25% more 16 to 19-year-olds looking for jobs in 1975 than there were in 1965 due to the rapid influx of people entering the labor market. This will occur as the blue-collar jobs for which they will be applying will be opening up at a pace of roughly 15% per year. In other words, there is a very real probability that many, possibly most, of the children of the poor will become the fathers and mothers of the poor. If that happened, America would have a hereditary underclass for the first time in its history. War and inflation were two factors in why these risky tendencies did not take off in the 1960s. A million new positions in the military sector and 700,000 new "jobs" in the armed services were created as a result of the country's sad involvement in the atrocities in Southeast Asia. Although the army did not literally take in the poor because 80 percent of those who were drafted had high school diplomas, it did reduce some of their competitiveness in the labor market. The labor market then became even more constrictive as a result of inflation after 1965, which was brought on by a $10 billion "mistake" in federal expenditure that was motivated by too optimistic predictions of a victory in the war in 1966.

What, however, are the acceptable replacements for the jobs caused by war and inflation now that Vietnam is at peace? A quietist administration won't have the answer to that question in terms of policy; instead, radical new initiatives will.

The president does occasionally acknowledge some of his rhetorical challenges, though. Nixon criticized the National Council on Urban Growth Policy's expansive proposal as being too timid in his Population Address to Congress in the summer of 1969. Hale Boggs, John Sparkman, and even a former Democratic presidential candidate were part of the commission, which John Tower, a Goldwater Republican, had stated that the country needed to create ten new cities with one million residents apiece and ten new towns with 100,000 residents. The president stated of the commission's recommendation, "But the total number of people who would be accommodated if even those bold plans were implemented is only twenty million —a mere one-fifth of the expected thirty-year increase," after noting that there will be 100 million more Americans by the year 2000, with three-quarters of them living in urbanized areas. (Italics inserted.)

So, Mr. Nixon is correct when he asserts that the housing crisis will worsen absent drastic reforms. When Nixon insists on how big the problem is and how much less his own administration is doing than Mr. Johnson, it is a way of suggesting that the failure of the 1949 Housing Act will last for fifty years, or until the year 2000. The president would have addressed the matter during the 1968 campaign by proposing that private industry complete the task for a profit. He faulted the committee for not going far enough, although it discovered that private construction of new towns and cities only happens in "rare cases." As these endeavors require a significant investment in social capital, unfettered capitalism will not make it.

In summary, there is strong evidence that housing poverty will worsen as the 1970s get underway and that the poor children of the previous decade will have more children and grow the size of the other America as parents in a struggling economy. Of course, such disasters are not predestined; they will be the outcome of political decisions. And even though the Nixon administration has made it quite clear that it does not comprehend the issue, it is nevertheless critical to briefly explain what has to be done.

Planning is necessary in the beginning. There should be a Joint Congressional Committee on the Future and an Office of the Future under the presidency that would receive, discuss, and approve or amend annual reports from the White House (I spelled out this suggestion in Toward a Democratic Left).

American ears would find this proposition weird, but there are evidence that moderates and even conservatives are starting to see its merits. In his Population Address, President Nixon raised the question of whether or not cities will be ready for an influx of 100 million new residents in the next 30 years. They are not, and a sharp rise in population will only make many issues worse, as evidenced by the chaotic history of urban growth. Later on, he got right to the point: "Maybe the most worrisome aspect of the current scenario is that so few individuals are looking at these concerns from the perspective of the entire society."

Precisely. Without giving the central city slum or the surrounding countryside a second thought, suburban home builders, car makers, and trucking firms all get their hefty federal subsidies. And right now, if poverty is to be eradicated as well as to prevent the quality of life in America from declining, we must adopt long-term priorities and pay even more attention to the "side effects" of new technologies than we do with new medications. Dwight Eisenhower advocated for the creation of new, integrated cities with new jobs a year before he passed away. Mr. Nixon seemed to concur. Yet, Adam Smith's "invisible hand" will not carry out the extraordinarily intricate planning required to complete such a task.

The second need is that social investments total billions of dollars.

President Nixon, like his predecessor President Johnson, believes that all of these difficulties can be resolved by enlisting the help of the private sector. When Mr. Nixon became president, he ordered that the "black capitalism" doctrine be applied to all the minority groups that were experiencing poverty. Yet, the harsh economic realities are that costs in the slums are twice as expensive as in the suburbs, traffic is much worse, and the labor market is comparatively untrained, i.e., all of the hardships that the country has placed on the poor make their communities unprofitable for big enterprise. Minority businesses can, of course, benefit their communities and should receive considerable support, but for the vast majority of people, there is little hope in them.

But as the 1960s came to a close, there did seem to be one area where public-private cooperation worked well: employment. With significant federal support, the National Association of Businessmen is working to place minority and low-income workers in rewarding positions. The progress that has been done has received a lot of media attention. A 1969 Wall Street Journal analysis, however, was less upbeat. According to Alan Otten, the tight labor market was a major factor in these hirings, and any increase in unemployment—which would inevitably occur given the Nixon approach to combat inflation—would force these people back onto the streets. However, the Ford Corporation rejected the Automobile Workers Union's request that older members be allowed to take a voluntary layoff so that the new men may remain on staff. The explanation was straightforward enough: Veteran unemployment benefits are more expensive than those for new hires. And the layoffs in the car industry started in the winter of 1970, specifically affecting the men who had been so enthusiastically recruited. Profit considerations trumped social concern.

Therefore, 100 million new Americans need new cities, and everyone needs access to good jobs.

will only occur if significant social investments are made. The United States' gross domestic output will surpass $1 trillion in the early 1970s. According to a Fortune article that analyzed this tendency, there would be a fiscal "dividend" of $38 billion in 1974 and around $80 billion by 1980. This is the automatic gain in government income that occurs when the GNP increases and does not involve any tax increases. Finding the resources is not the issue in this situation; the issue is having the intelligence to employ the resources democratically and inventively. To do that the nation should embrace the Economic Bill of Rights recommended by Martin Luther King Jr. in the last days of his life: every citizen has a right either to a decent work or to an appropriate income.

President Nixon launched a scathing critique of the current system of states' rights welfare in his welfare message from 1969. Yet, he advocated for Congress to grant even more authority to the local governments that had previously misused it in his good ideas, and he came out in favor of a federal minimum that would put most people well below the poverty line. The twenty states that currently pay less than that would only be needed to contribute half of their current welfare spending to the overall budget since Washington would supply the funding to raise family payments to $1,600 per year (and food stamps would add another $900).

The United States should adopt the notion that all of its residents are legally entitled to a fair income rather than institutionalizing a government minimum that is much below the poverty level. One such social investment, a negative income tax, was estimated by Lyndon Johnson's departing Cabinet to cost between $15 and $20 billion annually. With the

Fortune forecast of a $80 billion dividend by 1980, that sum is unquestionably within the realm of possibility for the nation.

Of course, there should be a work incentive in such a program. The welfare recipient should be permitted to keep a smaller fraction of his income supplement as his pay increases rather to the traditional American approach of taxing his earnings at a rate of 100% (by cutting his benefits by the amount of his wages). Yet this also implies that the number of respectable jobs must significantly expand. Mothers in New York City have no incentive to hunt for employment and haven't done so because Assistance for Dependent Children payments there are roughly equivalent to the income of low-wage jobs in the economy. Therefore, a commitment to actual full employment results from a guaranteed income with a work incentive.

And that is where the notion of a guaranteed income ties in with the right to work. Franklin Roosevelt was the one who initially argued, during the 1944 campaign, that if the private economy cannot give people jobs, then the public economy must. If we eventually implement this plan after a decade of unjustifiable deliberation, society would be able to exploit the vast untapped resource of the unemployed and underemployed to create a new, livable environment. If the Housing Acts of 1949 and 1968 were to live up to their promises, there would be a labor shortage and the nation would realize that the poor and the near poor are exactly who it needs. Additionally, because these workers would be generating worthwhile goods and services in exchange for their salary, the impact of such a program wouldn't be inflationary.

Hence, the 1970s require well-thought-out, long-term social investments to ensure that every person has a decent place to live and that everyone has access to a good job or a living wage. But as the decade gets underway, the country, including its leader, holds onto myths that prevent us from even describing the issue as it is. When we actually done so little, they believe we tried too much. Additionally, government statisticians and intellectuals are even eradicating poverty and making the impoverished invisible on paper.

Thus, there is justification for pessimism. Yet in order to stop these ominous trends, America must comprehend one important idea: that ending the anger of the impoverished is in the best interests of the entire society.

The most visible and painful victims of the economic and social trends that endanger the entire country are the poor. Millions of the wealthy are also impacted by the unplanned, chaotic urbanization that they suffer from the most. They are the first to see technological advancement as a curse that eliminates the traditional manual labor occupations that earlier generations relied on to claw their way out of poverty. But, the nature of labor is increasingly becoming a problem for the most advantaged members of society, as the current student radicalism makes obvious. In other words, if cities grow out of control and technology revolutionizes the land carelessly, polluting the very necessities of human existence like air and water, it will be the poor who suffer the greatest abuse while the entire country descends into decadence.

Every American should be dedicated to eradicating the other America out of moral and justifiable principles, as it is unthinkable that the richest country in human history could tolerate such senseless misery. But more than that, if we solve the problem of the other America we will have learnt how to tackle the problems of all of America.

POVERTY IN THE 1980s

The twentieth anniversary of the proclamation of an "unconditional war" against poverty in the United States was in January 1984. It is conceivable that when that anniversary comes around, poverty in the country will have become at least as entrenched as it was when President Johnson proclaimed that war. Moreover, it is not at all impossible that there will be more people living in the other America in the 1980s than in the 1960s. Under the best of circumstances, poverty will undoubtedly continue to be a serious issue in this nation.

This quick look back at events from the past two decades—this book was first published in 1962—is therefore more than just a historical study exercise. Instead, it is an effort to comprehend the past in order to control the future. The years since the declaration of the war on poverty have demonstrated that the core causes of the outrage of lack and even hunger in the richest society in the world are our institutional framework and everyday practices. So, more fundamental changes in economic and social policy are required than Johnson ever anticipated if the vision stated by President Johnson in 1964 is to be realized and poverty eradicated from this country.

Does this imply that since the early 1960s, nothing has been accomplished in this field? Not at all. As we will show, there have been significant improvements, especially between 1963 and 1969. Some of these improvements, like the reduction of senior citizen poverty, have persisted even today, despite the current threat of reversal. In order to avoid claiming that we were wholly unsuccessful, which would be false, I would instead argue that we overestimated the challenge we set for ourselves. It is crucial that we comprehend this point in order to avoid condemning ourselves and, more importantly, the poor, to yet another cycle of false hope and terrible disappointment if we ever put this subject back on the urgent agenda of the country, which I believe we will, though not in the near future.

This summary of the previous two decades will be produced in terms of three major topics. It will serve as the starting point for the following decade. There will first be an examination of how poverty, the economics, and political movements are related in the United States. The notion of poverty will next be closely scrutinized, especially in light of recent efforts to counter that we have overstated rather than understated the issue. Finally, a brief summary of prior initiatives will be given, along with an outlook on potential future steps that could genuinely end poverty in the United States.

It will be required to employ statistics and other forms of economic and social analysis to examine these issues. This must be done, not least because many people accuse those of us who speak out against the crime of poverty of speaking from a place of little thought and much emotion. It is even alleged that by sentimentally convincing people that there is a vast other America, we waste money on ineffective programs that could be implemented to address the nation's localized problem of poverty. Hence, in a way, those of us who consider the plight of the poor to be one of the major difficulties facing our society must present a "professional," emotionless argument for our position.

Following the release of all the statistics, the reader is advised to drive through almost any rural area in the country or take a stroll through any major American city in order to open their eyes to the hopeless and pinched faces of people who are compelled to live in intolerable conditions rather than the statistics. A fresh war against poverty has begun as a result of that existential realization, and perhaps poverty will prevail this time.

First things first: throughout the past 20 years, poverty in the United States has proven to be a dynamic phenomenon rather than a fixed one. The economic and political ups and downs that we experience greatly influence the fate of those who live in poverty.

During the longest stretch of prosperity in American history, the 1960s saw the rediscovery of poverty. Ironically, it was this relative prosperity—the emphasis should be on "relative," since the bulk of Americans have always had and still do struggle to make ends meet—that allowed us to once again perceive the impoverished. One factor was the perception that no one would have to make sacrifices in the fight against poverty. The Kennedy-Johnson years' New Economics doctrine claimed that the boom-bust economic cycle had come to an end. The government had figured out how to "fine-tune" the economy by just making minor changes to monetary policy and fiscal policy (the U.S. budget) (the Federal Reserve system and the Treasury). In order to make things clearer while still being fair, Washington would run a deficit and increase the money supply, which would generate the purchasing power needed to restart the economy. The Kennedy-Johnson tax cut's success appeared to provide empirical support for this strategy. By shifting some of the government's income to private consumers, the tax cut first decreased federal revenues. But, since those consumers helped the economy grow by spending money, Washington actually saw a rise in tax income; although its percentage of the pie was smaller, it was still a much larger pie overall.

Indeed, Daniel Patrick Moynihan, who had worked on that program under Johnson, stated that Washington was confronted with "a situation utterly without parallel in modern government: administrations that must be constantly on the lookout for new ways to expend public funds in the public interest" in a book on antipoverty policy that was published in 1969. Even though taxes had been reduced, the nation's constantly expanding gross domestic product would continue to bring in more and more money for the government. If Washington didn't use that money right away, it would reduce the economy's purchasing power and cause a downturn. Hence, efficient economic management needed investments in social justice, in stark contrast to the notion that government must be thrifty. During the Johnson administration, the president and some of the most influential figures in American business, like Henry Ford II, believed that a "partnership" between business and the federal government would be the most effective way to accomplish this. A Great Society would be created, the government would get the gratitude of the entire country, and the private sector would profit from developing affordable homes or offering subsidized education, training, and employment to the underprivileged.

If inflation were to ever become an issue, it would be handled with the same preciseness as unemployment. The government would cut expenditure, run a surplus, and raise taxes if too much money was chasing too few goods—the traditional definition of inflation. The Vietnam War caused that idyllic situation to start to fall apart. Lyndon Johnson was reluctant to raise taxes to pay for that unpopular intervention because he believed that one more round of escalation would put an end to the fight. The unemployment rate dropped to 3.8 percent in 1967, which was the lowest level since the end of World War II. Supposedly, now was the moment for fiscal restraint; nonetheless, Johnson ran a deficit of more than $12 billion in that year, primarily as a result of the Vietnam War. Therefore, inflation increased.

The true surprise, however, occurred when Richard Nixon became president two years later, in 1969. Nixon made the decision to battle the inflation brought on by the Vietnam War by causing a recession, acting in accordance with basic liberal doctrine. When the unemployment rate increased, prices remained unchanged. This was a first for us.

Stagflation, which is the prevalent economic reality today and defies all of these theories and "fine-tuning" measures, is characterized by simultaneous unemployment and high prices. The main sufferers of this unique reality were the impoverished. Every year throughout the Kennedy-Johnson era, official measures of poverty decreased. Due to the recession-inflation in 1970, the other America had its first expansion in ten years. Due to yet another recession-inflation (the worst since the Great Depression of the Thirties), it occurred once more in 1971, once in 1974, and once in 1975. It is currently occurring in 1980 as I write this Afterword.

The working poor are the most evident victims of the stagflation roller coaster. In 1976, 5.3 million families lived below the designated poverty threshold. The head of the family worked during the year in 2.45 million of those units, and in nearly one-fifth of them, they did so full-time. These are people with enormous families and obviously low-paying jobs. When a recession strikes, they either lose their jobs, which pushes them deeper into poverty, or their bargaining leverage for salaries, which is already limited because the majority of these workers are not unionized, is reduced. A group of laborers who are barely able to afford food is simultaneously pushed into the other America for the same reasons.

But, those who are not employed at all suffer as well. These are the dependent poor who rely heavily on government "transfer payments" (the formal term for funds received without payment for labor, commonly referred to as "welfare"). In reality, this group is much less than most people realize—only around 40% of impoverished families received public assistance in the middle of the 1970s—but it still contains roughly two million households, many of which are fairly large. There is a ton of evidence that throughout time, the government income that these people receive varies in line with economic fluctuations. Welfare payments are not increased while unemployment is high and working-class incomes are losing real purchasing power, as was the case in the "terrible" years of the 1970s and is still the case in the early 1980s. Politically and economically, the United States never lets such outlays get ahead of the market for menial, low-paying jobs. Indeed, in 1976 Charles Schultze, then at the Brookings Institution and later chairman of the President's Council of Economic Advisers, warned Congress that if it legislated a right to a well-paid job in the public sector for everyone who could not find one in the private sector, it would undercut all the low-paying industries. The legislators and entrepreneurs find this point to be much more appealing when it comes to giving assistance payments to folks who aren't even looking for work.

Only one subset of the poor did not experience the stagflation's ills as severely as the others, though this may alter in the future. Benefits from Social Security are "indexed," meaning on a regular basis, they are automatically increased to reflect changes in the cost of living. The number of the elderly poor as a percentage of all Americans over 65 has decreased by roughly half as a result of the Social Security benefits being increased in the 1960s and 1970s. Hence, the indexing and higher benefits shielded this strata from the economic injustices that befell both the working poor and the welfare poor.

Nonetheless, there are grounds for some skepticism in this regard. Since more taxpayers lost their jobs during the recession of 1974–1975, Washington received significantly less money from the Social Security tax than usual. It is important to keep in mind that the Social Security system is not "financed," meaning that the money that people contribute is not put into investments to cover their eventual retirement. When the former are old enough, a still younger generation will finance their retirement. Now, the Social Security taxes of the working-age generation are used to pay the pensions of those in retirement. So, a recession lowers the funds available for retirees, and a stagflation recession raises the amount that must be paid out to them due to the high prices that go along with it. As a result of declining earnings and increasing commitments, the system experienced a crisis in the middle of the 1970s.

In light of these facts, President Ford suggested a 5 percent "cap" on Social Security indexing. That meant that retirees would only be paid for 5% of their lost purchasing power if prices increased by more than 13% in a single year, as they did in 1975. So, a president of the United States was advocating for a decrease in the real quality of life for those over 65. This similar notion was now put forth from the middle of the political spectrum during the discussions over balancing the budget in 1980. So, if the economy continues to deteriorate in the 1980s, there are alarming reasons to believe that the elderly poor will no longer be partly insulated from the increase in poverty that affected other age groups during the difficult years of the 1970s.

In assessing the destiny of the various strata of the other America, I have employed the convenient measurements of income and buying power in order to determine their respective places. But there is another, extremely significant aspect of the problem that was evident during the 1970s decade. When unemployment and poverty rise, societal pathology—such as alcoholism, drug addiction, family disintegration, and crime— also rises. In 1962, I wrote about this phenomenon in The Other America; sadly, it has persisted in essentially the same form ever since. When considering racial concerns in the US, this is very troubling. As just one-third of the poor are black, and two-thirds are white, poverty is not primarily a problem of race. The fact that black Americans make up one-third of the poor and slightly more than 10% of the population as a whole is undoubtedly racist. But, this does not imply that one may compare racial inequality to poverty.

Racist effects of the economy are particularly pronounced in one specific sector, though. In the 1970s, the unemployment rate among young blacks and Hispanics living in the slums frequently reached 40 or 50 percent, exceeding the rate seen by Americans during the Great Depression in the 1930s. These young people are prevented from entering the workforce at the point when they would typically make their first acquaintance with the working world. Even if it is already unpleasant when it occurs, this is a potentially deadly sign of things to come. Because they are almost guaranteed to contribute a disproportionate amount of the 1980s' violent offenders and muggers if there is a sizable and considerable group of young poor people who are abandoned on the social scrap heap while they are in their teens. In other words, society will tragically pay a price for its callousness. Incidentally, it is more expensive to keep someone in jail than to send them to Harvard.

Political trends are not produced by these economic and social movements alone. For instance, Richard Nixon plainly believed that he had the authority to completely dismantle what little the anti-poverty campaign had left when he assumed office in 1969. But several 1960s programs had begun to attract a political audience. There were mayors of large cities, for example, who took an interest in various employment training programs. Hence, even though the tone changed in the 1970s, the programs of the 1960s did not terminate abruptly. Even the vast power of the presidency was thwarted by a political lag that had institutionalized in such a way.

Yet as the 1970s went on, that delay started to matter less and less. Hence, political and ideological tendencies, as well as economic developments, must be included among the factors that influence poverty in the United States. A definite shift to the right in the country was the initial reaction to stagflation. By the way, that's in keeping with a long-standing custom. During bad times, each person seeks to save himself or herself and there is a puzzled rejection of any type of collective solution. The gains of the New Deal in the thirties did not come in 1932 under Hoover, when the Depression was at its worst, or even in 1933 under Roosevelt, but in 1935 and 1936, when there was an improvement in the economy and Americans once again afforded themselves the luxury of hope.

The rediscovery of poverty also occurred during a period of relative prosperity and decreased unemployment, as we have already mentioned. Again, it wasn't a natural outcome of the happy times. For instance, it is almost probable that the rise in social consciousness in the early 1960s would not have happened if it weren't for Martin Luther King Jr. and the movement he helped form. One of the most charismatic Americans to have ever lived spearheaded a massive, nonviolent movement in this nation beginning with the Montgomery Bus Boycott in 1955. King did not, in those early years, speak of the poverty of black America. He instead focused on legal discrimination, particularly the denial of the right to vote and of access to public places. But it was nonetheless undeniable that the blacks who followed Dr. King came from the country's lowest neighborhoods and social strata. The moral and political pressure of the civil rights movement helped to propel the government in the direction of doing something about poverty, even with a young and liberal president in the White House—another political variable.

In fact, it is obvious that those same variables also influenced how this novel turned out. The impact of The poor policies in America would not have been as great if it had been released five years sooner or one year later. Yet it was revealed at the same time when the young president was reacting to both the Dr. King-led black uprising and the realization that the unemployment rate was more difficult to solve than he had anticipated. Kennedy inquired about the book's contents after learning about it from the head of the Council of Economic Advisers. When informed that there was, the president read it. According to Arthur Schlesinger's administration history, this reading contributed to the president's decision to make poverty a priority. The aim is not to delve into the details of this historical footnote, but rather to provide another another illustration of how broader political and economic circumstances influence how we see poverty.

The political climate in the 1970s and the early 1980s was completely different from that of the 1960s. Stagflation subverted the black movement, which was in chaos and had not even started to find a replacement for Martin Luther King Jr.

The original impulse was to turn back to Herbert Hoover rather than look much further than Lyndon Johnson and John F. Kennedy, which was liberal wisdom of the 1960s. Undoubtedly, the situation did not just rush to the right. As noted by Everett C. Ladd, a politically conservative political scientist, different surveys conducted in the late 1970s revealed that the public was more conservative in general and extremely liberal in particular. In other words, they supported philosophic claims about the inefficiency and wastefulness of government engagement in the economy while simultaneously calling for increased government involvement in issues like unemployment, the environment, health care, and other similar ones. There was, however, one notable exception: people were very conservative when it came to "welfare," or taking action to combat poverty.

This trend was made stronger by the belief of some analysts that demographics would resolve the issue of poverty in the 1980s.

The massive increase in births that the returning war veterans started in the late 1940s and continued into the early 1960s, known as the "postwar baby boom," will have come to an end in the labor market by 1985. At that point, there will be a reduced labor force and the number of new workers entering the workforce each year will start to fall. Given all else being equal, this implies that the unemployment issue will be simpler to solve and that poverty, as it pertains to joblessness, will decrease. Nevertheless, nothing is ever equal. One reason is that over the past ten years, the "full employment-unemployment rate," which is our official measure of how well we are doing in this area, has been continuously rising. According to John F. Kennedy, full employment was reached when the unemployment rate reached 3%; Lyndon Johnson increased that to 4%; Nixon-Ford and Jimmy Carter set it at about 5%; and in 1980, one of the country's top economists, Martin Feldstein, suggested that the rate could reach 8 or 9 percent in the Wall Street Journal. Inflation starts when that rate is attained, and the government moves to reduce expenditures.

In other words, it is official doctrine that for the American economy to function "normally," there must be about 5 million unemployed people (or about 5% unemployment in a labor force of nearly 100 million people), and it is unofficially estimated that there must be 7 to 19 million unemployed people for things to proceed smoothly. According to that statistical definition, there is a significant proportion of poverty that is "justifiable" in prosperous times. The unemployment rate did not grow over 5.9 percent during the Nixon recession of 1969–1971, which sparked the first increase in the other America in ten years and is today regarded as being at, or even below, "full employment."

If one thinks that the 1980s will likely experience challenging economic conditions and insufficient political responses, at least in the first years of the decade, as I have argued in Decade of Decision: The Crisis of the American System, one comes to a pessimistic conclusion about the future of the poor. Given those circumstances, there may very well be more people living in poverty in 1984 than there were in 1964, when Lyndon Johnson proclaimed a "unconditional war" against it.

There are some serious and knowledgeable people who claim that all of the statistics I've used to support this claim are greatly inflated and that the actual magnitude of the poverty issue is less than we think, not greater.

I set a rather arbitrary threshold for poverty at a yearly income of $3,000 in the late 1950s. Following Johnson's program announcement, the federal government undertook the task of developing a thorough definition of the phrase, which was later utilized in legislation. At the Social Security Administration, Molly Orshansky created the new, more exact notion. Based on a 1955 research that revealed families spent one-third of their money on food, Orshansky multiplied the cost of the

Department of Agriculture's economy food plan—the least expensive nutritionally sound food budget—by three. A family was deemed to be poor if it had less than three times the amount needed for that low food expenditure. The economic food plan's price was updated to account for price changes, but not its nutritional makeup, and the metric was modified for family size. There is not, therefore, one poverty "line" in the United States, but a number of poverty lines that vary by family size and, to a certain extent, by geographic area. The poverty "line" for farm families, who are assumed to grow some of their own food, is between 70 and 85% of the corresponding nonfarm level.

The statisticians followed the politicians during the rightward movement in the 1970s as was previously discussed. I'm not recommending a scheme; I'm just making the case that in the 1960s, a researcher got recognition for bringing attention to the poverty we had overlooked, and in the 1970s, praise went to those who discovered the poverty we had exaggerated. Anderson is an academic conservative, and the (Herbert) Hoover Institution released his book in the proper manner. The Congressional Budget Office (CBO) made even a more serious attack on the poverty notion, since it is legislatively supposed to be impartial and was, at the time of the attack, under the guidance of a liberal economist, Alice Rivlin.

The primary argument made by the CBO was that the government's definition of poverty was solely dependent on financial circumstances. That, however, disregarded the enormous growth in "in kind" programs, in which recipients were given free or heavily discounted goods or services rather than cash. The two most significant examples are food and health (Medicare for the elderly and Medicaid for some of the poor) (food stamps). Around one-third of American poverty was eliminated when the financial worth of these "in kind" programs—valued by the amount the federal government paid for them—was added to their meager income. This argument was put out by certain liberals. They claimed that by exaggerating poverty, one could persuade people that government activity in this area was unsuccessful and provide justification for a cut in spending rather than an increase.

Most of what the CBO indicated would be convincing if it had been presented as "in kind" income as part of a fair characterization of poverty. One could still challenge some of the assumptions—for instance, do the poor genuinely receive health care comparable to the cost of Medicaid, or isn't it possible that part of that money is improperly and ineffectively spent or even ripped off? Yet, the fundamental idea would be quite valid. But after that, one would also look into any and all instances of undercounting and overcounting. For instance, the number of "undocumented" workers in the United States is enormous (mainly Mexicans in the Southwest and people from the Caribbean in the Southeast and Northeast). As they do not want to be identified by any governmental agency, they are not included in any of our statistics. There may be up to 10 million persons who were undercounted in the census for this group. Even though the majority of these folks are poor, they do not fulfill any of our standards and primarily do not receive any "in kind" benefits.

The initial definition was deemed inadequate by Molly Orshansky and others for a variety of technical factors (not only is it necessary to upgrade the cost of the economy meal, but the character of the meal itself should be redefined). Unrelated to that, more Americans agree with Orshansky than the CBO. When pollsters ask respondents to define poverty, the responses are remarkably consistent: most individuals place the "line" at 50% of the median income. (Median income is the population's fiftyth percentile's value.

i.e., half the population has more than the median and half has less.) The poverty "line" for a family of four living in an urban area in 1977 was $6,191; nevertheless, the "line," as the average American would understand it, would have been at $8,613 in that year for families earning half the median income.

I made the case that 40 to 50 million Americans lived in poverty using shoddy government statistics and a lot of gut feeling. When the government learned more about the issue, it calculated that there were around 39.5 million people living in poverty in 1959, the year on which the majority of my data is based. In essence, it found that my lower prediction had been roughly accurate. Under the same standard, Washington estimated that around 25 million Americans were living in poverty in 1976. According to the CBO, this number approximately exaggerated poverty by 35%. But if one agrees with my criticism of the CBO, there are not fewer impoverished people, but rather more than the government says. And if the prior analysis is accurate, due to economic and political factors, there will be even more in the early 1980s. Whereas the government estimated that 13.5% of families were considered to be poor in 1976, and the CBO reported that the real number was 8.3%, I believe it was closer to 20%.

But does it imply that I am making the case that all prior federal initiatives were unsuccessful, as some CBO supporters claim?

And if that's the case, how does one come up with a plan to eradicate poverty in the future?

To start, some of the earlier efforts were successful. During the Kennedy-Johnson era, a sizable portion of the working poor were able to transcend poverty thanks to eight years of consistently declining unemployment. Of course, the 1970s—during the administrations of Nixon, Ford, and Carter—as well as the 1980s—show that rising unemployment causes people to fall into the category of the working poor. Nonetheless, we are aware that there is room for improvement in this area, and I'll come back to that. There were other initiatives as well that had an impact. The most prominent example is the food stamp program. Spending in this sector progressively rose, serving as an illustration of a program that is really federal and effective. ("Welfare," primarily Aid for Families of Dependent Children, and Medicaid are partially funded by Washington but designed by the states, meaning that there are significant differences in terms of eligibility and benefit levels; food stamps are distributed uniformly, in accordance with federal criteria.) The 1960s' employment training initiatives met with varying degrees of success. The same is true in regards to educational spending. (These judgments are documented in The Promise of Greatness, by Sar Levitan and Robert Taggart, and by Henry Aaron in Politics and the Professors: The Great Society in Context.) However, both Social Security payment increases and their indexation have significantly reduced the poverty rate for those over 65.

Consequently, I am not suggesting that all of the 1960s projects were a failure; rather, I am stating that the issues they addressed proved to be more complicated and deeply ingrained in our institutions than had been anticipated. It would have been quite simple to abolish the majority of poverty if the ecstatic hopes of the Kennedy-Johnson years had come true and the gross national product had expanded continuously with stable prices. (But not all; large families with a female head of household exacerbated their poverty in both prosperous and difficult times.) But such dreams were crushed, and the fundamental tendencies of the American economy toward boom and bust are to blame for that development. Hence, it is obvious that this nation must address the issue of stagflation, which does not seem impending in the early 1980s, if the poor are to be freed from their suffering.

There is a similar challenge. Richard Nixon gave the Washington Star a protracted interview the day following the 1972 election. In it, he made the well-known and highly popular claim that the 1960s "threw money at problems," or extravagant expenditure for the underprivileged that, on the whole, was ineffective. As we've seen, some of the programs were successful; for example, the elderly now enjoy considerably more comfortable lives thanks to the straightforward measure of raising their earnings. Throwing money at a problem is an effective strategy when people experience a severe lack of income. More significant, though, is the pervasive overestimation of funds allocated to the underprivileged. Henry Aaron has demonstrated that the inventions of the 1960s really gave the non-poor more money than the poor (federal subsidies to college education are a dramatic illustration). And according to Charles Schultze's calculations, the amount of real output that the federal government spent between the presidencies of Eisenhower and Carter, or more than 25 years, has not increased.

Two-thirds of all new federal spending in the 1960s went to Social Security and Medicare, the only group that did receive large increases from Washington during this time. But the majority of people are sympathetic toward this group precisely because they will eventually join it. So, when one looks at the truly controversial programs—aid to minorities, to slum communities, and the like—they did not receive anything at all. They increased by $35 billion, or 1.7 percent of the GDP, between 1965 and 1977, according to Charles Schultze's estimate. That amount is not significant, and in any case, the non-poor received a lot more. This problem is complicated in part by Lyndon Johnson's verbose style. Johnson once spoke as though his government was starting over every morning. They exaggerated the failures of those years because they inflated the expenditures, but it didn't.

But how can we get rid of the ludicrous paradox of extreme human need in a reasonably wealthy country, presuming that at some point in the 1980s, the topic of poverty would once again be on the pressing political agenda? The analysis I did has an implied answer to that query. The first and primary requirement for eradicating poverty is full employment, which should be seen as workers actively seeking employment, as it was during World War II, rather than as the extremely high level of tolerated unemployment as it is today. When unemployment was at 1% during World War II, blacks and women made the largest relative gains ever. Full employment would enable us to end the poverty of the working poor through the labor market and would provide the economic and political foundation for addressing the poverty of those outside of the labor market.

Second, by raising Social Security benefits to the point where they leave no one with an income deficit, we could completely eradicate the lingering financial poverty among the elderly.

Finally, a dedication to planned development of viable neighborhoods for everyone in the society is necessary to combat the most pervasive poverty in the nation—that of the fatherless families in the slums and ghettoes. So, the current devastation of large portions of the major Northeast cities and the industrial Middle West must be prevented. Full employment policies would be crucial in this situation as well, for example, by placing a government-owned solar energy plant in the middle of a damaged neighborhood or by building new communities on both new and existing property.

As my position has already been made clear enough, I won't go into more detail here. On the one hand, compared to the relatively affluent 1960s, when the economic indicators obediently behaved as the economic theories stated they should, the issues of a stagflationist economy are unprecedented and make the eradication of poverty more challenging. On the other hand, there are initiatives that, in particular, a planned economy with full employment, might enable the end all these, once and for all. But, in order for those programs to be successful, rather drastic new policy changes are needed, policies that go beyond the liberalism of Franklin Roosevelt and Lyndon Johnson in the same way that their liberalism went beyond Hoover's conservatism. With the revelation of poverty twenty years ago, it has become clear that this indignation is far more institutional and structural than we ever imagined. There is no way that the regular operations of the 1970s would have put an end to poverty in the 1980s.

I'll therefore end this review on a mixed note. There has been progress; further progress is possible; and the poor don't have to stay with us forever. To achieve that advancement, however, political groups will need to be both more creative and aggressive than those that existed in 70s and 80s.

NOTES:

NOTES:

NOTES:

Made in United States
Orlando, FL
08 April 2023

31907152R00041